Encounters With Angels

Gail Y. Taliaferro

Encounters With Angels
Copyright © 2015
Gail Y. Taliaferro
ISBN: 978-1-946180-02-5

Gail Y. Taliaferro
Feed My Lambs Ministries, Int'l.
918-698-4461
tgtali@aol.com
www.facebook.com/gytaliaferro

Cover and Text Design:
www.SimpsonProductions.net

All rights reserved.
Printed in the United States of America.
To reproduce this book in any form,
please contact the Author.

Dedication

I dedicate this book to my mother and father,
Henry and June Taliaferro, who provided
a wonderful life for me and are now
with the angels in heaven.

There are different types of Angels.

Some have wings, some do not.
Angels take on human form.
Some angels sing.
Some angels play instruments.
Angels can drive.
There are warring angels.
There are angels that bring messages.
Angels are different nationalities.
You could be entertaining Angels unaware!

Contents

Introduction 9

1 Trip from Nigeria to USA 11

2 And Then There Were Six 13

3 Crusade in Nigeria 15

4 First Tulsa Apartment 17

5 ORU Swim Final 19

6 Baby's Guardian Angel 21

7 On the Road to Branson 25

8 Dream in Nigeria 29

9 DC to Tulsa Flight 2012 31

10 Broken Arrow Backyard 33

11 Choir Rehearsal 35

Conclusion 37

About the Author 38

Introduction

Definition: an-gel (noun)

- ❖ A spiritual being that serves as a messenger from God or as a guardian of human beings.

- ❖ A white-robed winged figure of human form.

- ❖ A spiritual being superior to humans in power and intelligence.[1]

Angels are mentioned in the Holy Bible from Genesis to Revelation. They are present in all types of situations.

This book is an account of the personal encounters I have had with angels thus far.

In the 1980's, people were writing books and talking on television talk shows about all their angelic visitations.

I have been in meetings where ministers of the gospel like Kenneth E. Hagin, Sr., Gloria Copeland and Richard Roberts

---

[1] Merriam-Webster. https://www.merriam-webster.com/dictionary/angel.

would see angels enter the room, take seats in the meetings and line up against the walls. WOW! I wanted to see them too!

I asked God, "Can I see an angel? Please, Lord, can I see an angel? Just one little angel, God? Please, can I see an angel? I gave up house and lands to follow You as a missionary. P-l-e-a-s-e can I see an angel?" That desire burning in my heart never let up, but I also never received an answer until . . .

One day I was on an airplane (where I knew I was close to headquarters), and I asked again, "God, can I please see an angel?" He immediately replies, "You'll see one when you need one."

How many of you know that when God speaks, it is settled? I NEVER asked again. I was at peace. I knew I would see one. Just never imagined how many I would see.

This book is an account of the encounters I personally have had with angels.

Fasten your seat belts; we are going for a ride!

1
Trip from Nigeria to USA

It was at the end of July. Word of Faith schools were out for the holidays, and Daisy and Freda Idahosa and I were ready for our vacation.

Margaret Idahosa, the Archbishop Benson A. Idahosa's wife, always had her big CWFI Convention for Women in August, but we didn't want to stay around for that so we secretly prayed and prayed that they would allow us to go to the USA by ourselves.

That was a big responsibility for me to take the girls overseas, but we were together a lot; and to our surprise they agreed to let us go. They called us into the sitting room, gave us a lecture and our individual envelopes of spending money for the month, prayed for us and we were off on our trip.

We entered the plane and sat down, Freda on the left side, me in the middle and Daisy on the right. We were fastening our seat belts when Freda screamed, "Auntie, look at the window." All three of us turned and looked, and there was a snow white, huge, glistening feather-like wing right outside the airplane!

We all saw it and knew it was an angel wing, and Freda said matter of factly, "Oh, that's just Mom and Dad praying for us!" We laughed, fastened our seat belts and began our wonderful trip.

It gave me great comfort to know that we had an angel assigned to us for the trip.

How special and grown-up we all felt, and what a wonderful time we all had.

Thank You, Lord, for divine protection.

2
And Then There Were Six

My first time flying alone to Nigeria had its own set of anxieties. Are my bags underweight? Will I get through immigration? Will someone be there to help me with my bags, pick me up at the airport in Lagos and finally get to Benin?

Pastors had prayed for me, and I was confident that Jesus was with me and everything would be all right.

The flight took off normally. We all settled in for a nice long flight. The stewardesses had completed the beverage service and had started the dinner service. I remember the stewardess was serving the people across the aisle from me when the plane suddenly just dropped.

Not a bump, not turbulence, but a significant drop. Food trays went flying in the air, people started screaming. Some called on Jesus. Some called on Allah. And some said some words I will not write in this book!

The stewardess fell over the arm of the chair, and I laid my head on the back of my seat and closed my eyes. When I opened my eyes, immediately I saw six angels, three on each side of the plane holding it in the air. A sigh of relief and a peace came over me. The four angels on the ends had wings, and the two in the middle did not. I have often drawn that picture and even had an artist draw it for me. I will never forget those six angels.

My pastor, Archbishop Benson Idahosa, always confidently said, "No plane that I am on can ever crash." He said he had not finished his work, and I was just starting mine.

Thank You, Lord, for Your divine protection.

3
Crusade in Nigeria

Church of God Mission International went to so many crusades in nine years. I can't remember where this one was, but I certainly remember what happened. I think it was in the North of Nigeria.

The crusade was about to start and people were walking from everywhere as usual to the crusade ground. I was walking among them when we came to a ravine. There was a river with rushing water with only a wooden plank for all these people to get across to the other side.

People were going across in an orderly fashion, but I was too scared to cross. As I got closer I could hear the water, and I said, "God, I can't cross this! The crowd will push me over."

Just as I got to the plank, a black man all dressed in a white agbada (an African free-flowing outer garment worn by men) got in front of me, and said, "Hold on." I grabbed on to the back of his clothes tightly with my eyes closed and was able to follow his footsteps on the plank of wood over the rushing river safely to the other side.

When I turned around to thank the kind man for helping me, he was back on the other side of the river. As he walked away he smiled and waved good-bye to me.

Oh, my God. It was a BLACK angel. Glory!!

Remember, God said to me, "You will see one when you need one."

God keeps His promises.

I cannot tell you how excited I get as I recall these angelic accounts. It's like they happened yesterday.

4
First Tulsa Apartment

I arrived in Tulsa, Oklahoma, for the first time in 1986 to attend Oral Roberts University's Master's Program in Educational Administration.

I knew I was covered in prayer by my Pastors, Archbishop Benson and Margaret Idahosa, as well as my mother, June Taliaferro, and a host of friends. However, I was still nervous about living in an apartment in a city where I didn't know anyone.

I never slept with alarm clocks because I didn't like the way they jolted me awake. So I always asked God to wake me up on time and He always did. But one morning I heard two distinct rapid knocks on my bedroom door. Thud! Thud!

From then on, every morning I would hear these two knocks waking me up at the proper time. Then one morning as I sat in the living room, I heard wings flapping away from my front door. Oh my!!!! Angels were assigned to my front door during the night and they left in the morning. Thank You, Jesus!

I heard them almost every morning for a very long time. I never saw them. It was very comforting.

I never thanked the angels or God or people who prayed for me for sending those angels to watch over me at that time.

Thank You, God. Thank you, everyone, who prayed those angels in for me.

5
ORU Swim Final

When you attended Oral Roberts University in the 1980's, you could not graduate without passing a Swimming Test. I do not know what the rules are today. No matter your grade point average or any disability, you had to take a modified test.

Everyone had several opportunities to take this test, and of course, I chose the last day of the five times you could take the test in my class due to intense fear.

You had to jump in the deep end, 12 feet, swim to the other end, turn over on your back and swim backwards back to the deep end in front of the instructor.

The last day of class I called my mother to pray with me before I went to take this test, and she prayed such a long prayer I looked at the clock and I was going to be late for class. I grabbed my swimming clothes bag and my book bag and ran out of the door in the winter.

Near ORU if you were walking, many times other students would offer you a ride. I was desperate. I needed a ride. I prayed. Suddenly a small red Fiat pulled up beside me. Two very Scandinavian looking guys with blond hair were in the car. They asked me where I was going. I said, "ORU." They didn't know where it was so I got in, which I would normally never do, and directed them to the campus.

As soon as I got in the car, I was overtaken by the anointing on these two men. I asked them who they were and what did they do, and the guy in the passenger seat just looked at me. He had a clipboard in his hands, and I could see big green check marks. They talked to each other in a different language. Never to me.

When we got up the hill on ORU's campus across from the pool, the man in the passenger seat got out. He was so tall I don't know how he fit into that small car! His hair was so blond. He gave me my swim bag and my book bag, and when I turned around to thank them, the car and the men were GONE!! Hallelujah! I thought, *if God could send angels to take me to the test, surely I have the courage to go in there and take the test.*

Thank You, Jesus! Again, I saw two when I needed them!

By the way, I passed the test. I graduated. Hallelujah!

6

Baby's Guardian Angel

When I was a Youth Pastor in Colmar Manor, Maryland, I was the youngest of seventeen ministers in that church.

The saddest funeral I have ever attended was where a beautiful eleven pound baby boy died in delivery.

The church was packed. Everyone in the church was sobbing. The father of the child brought in the tiny white casket under his arm followed by his six brothers.

The baby had on a white tuxedo trimmed in satin. His head was full of curly black hair. The men stood over the casket all crying.

The Pastor, my mother and everyone on the pulpit were weeping. I sat on the back row of the ministers on the pulpit praying, "God, send help from the sanctuary! Who is going to be able to preside over this funeral?"

Suddenly a large transparent angel flew into the room and took its position over the casket, remaining in the ceiling. Half of his body from his head to waist was against the ceiling and his lower body waist to feet hung straight down in a "L" shape. He stayed at attention in that position for the entire funeral. I kept peeking to see if he was still there. He never moved from that spot.

I never said anything in the funeral because I didn't want to scare people and I didn't want them to think I was carried away by emotion.

When we arrived where the repass was being held, I told the Pastor and she said I should have stood up and shared what I saw, that it would have comforted the people. I asked her if I could tell the parents, and she said, "Tell the grandmother and see if she gives you permission to tell the parents."

The grandmother was my secretary in the school, so I took her into a quiet room and told her. She said, "Yes, you can tell them," and so we brought the parents in. When we told them, the angel came into the room with us. When I finished telling them, the angel left, and I said, "Did you see the angel?" All three of them looked at each other and said, "No." I'm the only one who saw him again.

When we went to the cemetery, I walked the father to the gravesite. He said he didn't think he could do it. I said, "We can do it together." When we got to the spot, I looked at the sign. The cemetery area was called "The Guardian Angel plot."

I still shake as I write this.

7
On the Road to Branson

For several years now I have made the journey to Dr. Billye Brim's Prayer Conferences. This particular time I was making the journey alone for the first time, because the people I usually traveled and stayed with went two days earlier than I could get time off at work. So this experience happened on a Friday. I am sorry that I don't remember what year.

I left work around three o'clock (teaching in Tulsa Public schools at the time) to make the four-hour road trip from Tulsa to Branson, Missouri, headed for Chateau on the Lake Hotel to be there for the start of the meeting at seven o'clock.

I was very apprehensive because I had never driven there alone before, I didn't have GPS the way we do now and I was on a tight time schedule and didn't want to drive in the dark.

Both my friends whom I was sharing a room at the hotel with were checked in and already enjoying the meetings. I knew they were praying for me to get there.

As I am praying and driving, I asked God to send me a car with a bumper sticker or something that I could just follow to the hotel. No help.

I pulled into the gas station to refuel, and there was a man in a checkered shirt and a white baseball cap filling his car with gasoline. I asked him if I was going in the right direction for Chateau on the Lake Hotel. He said, "Yes." He was going that way and he could show me the way as far as he was going. Whew, was I relieved. God had answered my prayer.

Up to this point, I had been driving on the highway making good time, but this man began going the scenic route off the beaten path. We were going up and down hills, passing beautiful farms and crops. It was a beautiful view, but why were we not speeding down the highway! I had to check in and get to the meeting!

Finally, we came to a stop. The sun was going down. It was getting dark, and the man says, "This is as far as I go." Then he asked me if I enjoyed the scenery because he wanted to show me the beautiful countryside. I said, "Yes, it was very nice." Then he proceeded to give me the strangest directions I have ever received.

He said, "Just follow the North Star and keep the moon on your left behind your shoulder." What? He was giving me directions from the sky? A heavenly perspective. All of a sudden it was like my understanding was awakened. Is he an angel?

While the man was talking to me, his arms were folded leaning in the driver's side window of my car; and when I put my hand out to touch him to see if he was real, he jumped back. He stared at me, and said, "The bumper sticker on your car says, "Angels watching over me," doesn't it?

I sat there staring at him as he backed away from the car, and as I drove away he stared at me. Ahhhhhhhhhhhhhh!!! I screamed and shook as I drove off.

Again, I remembered, "You'll see one when you need one."

I followed the star and kept the moon on my left, and soon I saw the hotel shining in the distance on top of the hill.

I couldn't wait to tell my roommates how I got there, or do I tell anyone?

8
Dream in Nigeria

One afternoon I had a dream. I do not dream often, so I take my dreams very seriously.

I dreamt I was in the Idahosa family's black SUV with their children and the driver going somewhere in town.

As we were traveling along, I saw a disturbance ahead of us. There were lots of men in the intersection with machetes and planks ready to hurt someone. They were screaming and shouting.

I screamed to the driver to stop and turn around. I did not want us to go through them. The driver just kept driving. The closer we got to the angry mob, the more frightened I became. I jumped out of the car and the car kept going.

Immediately when I jumped down from the car, two big black angels with full armor and huge swords flew into the intersection.

The one in front told me to stand to the side. His voice was like thunder. He spoke the word, "Peace." I saw peace come out of his mouth like ripples on a pond and quiet came over the street that had been in chaos. The car with the children went safely through the crowd, and I woke up.

I ran, got dressed and went to the main house to tell Bishop Margaret Idahosa what I had dreamed. She asked me, "Gail, do you know who those men were?" I said, "Yes, Ma'am." They were angels. Big black warring angels this time.

Again, you'll see one when you need one!

9
DC to Tulsa Flight 2012

On one of my many flights to Tulsa, Oklahoma, I was quietly resting on our journey. While looking out the window, suddenly I saw the tallest, most magnificent angel I had ever seen just standing on a cloud in mid air outside the plane.

I gasped with excitement, shook my head and blinked my eyes to make sure I wasn't dreaming.

Suddenly seated about three rows ahead of me on the plane, I heard two children scream, "Mommy, there's an angel!" Thank You, Lord, for the confirmation.

To my dismay I heard the mother say, "Oh, there's no angel out there," and then I heard a pop. She had hit one of them or both, I don't know. I couldn't see.

(Parents, listen. When your children tell you things, sometimes they see things we don't see.)

The angel was transparent with the biggest, most beautiful lace-like wings, again standing out there on assignment watching the plane. The angel did not move, and the cloud did not appear to be moving.

What a magnificent creature! So beautiful. So tall. And children could see him as well.

Thank You, Lord, for opening our eyes to see.

Thank You for giving me this quiet time and a safe place to write.

10
Broken Arrow Backyard

I was blessed to live a year-and-a-half in my dream house in Broken Arrow, Oklahoma.

One afternoon, pastor friends of mine Howard and Cheryl, who were in Tulsa visiting for Word Explosion at Victory Christian Center, came by for a visit.

They had been wonderful Care Pastors to me, and I wanted to show them my new home. While his wife, Cheryl, was upstairs with me in the prayer room, I didn't realize Howard was walking through the house praying by himself.

When he came back upstairs to join us, he waited until we finished talking, and then asked, "Gail, did you know there is a big angel standing under the tree in your backyard? He's big!"

My eyes got big. I said, "No."

"Well, there is," he said. "He's just standing there so you do not have to fear." Glory!!!!!!!

After that, every time I passed the sliding door to the backyard, I would open it and say, "Good morning" or "Good night, sir."

Thank God for angelic protection!

Do you know you have angels watching over you?

11
Choir Rehearsal

One Thursday night we were in choir rehearsal, and the presence of God just fell on the choir. People were crying and worshipping God. Some knelt on the ground, some with uplifted hands, some lay prostrate on the floor. As I looked up, the ceiling of the church opened up, and I saw in a circle the sky with clouds behind it and angels looking into the church.

Some were just watching; others had long golden horns and they were playing with the worship we were offering. I quietly went over to the Music Director and told her what I saw, and she said, "You should tell Pastor. It would bless her."

I will never forget the night God opened my eyes to see the angels come to worship with us.

Conclusion

In this season God is releasing people to tell of their experiences because it is Time for the Supernatural!

I have included references to Angels in the Bible so you will know Angels are real.

God bless you and know that Angels are watching over you.

Gail

About the Author

Gail Yvonne Taliaferro is an Ordained Minister, Missionary, Psalmist, Educator, Conference Speaker and Author.

She was born to Henry and June Taliaferro in Washington, DC, where she attended public schools. She has a younger brother named Guy.

She received her B.A. in Music Education from Bennett College in Greensboro, North Carolina, and a Master's Degree in Educational Administration from Oral Roberts University in Tulsa, Oklahoma. She recently graduated from Victory Bible College in Tulsa, Oklahoma.

Gail spent ten years in Benin City, Nigeria, serving as an Education Administrator, establishing over 36 Christian schools; and Music Missionary and lecturer in the Faculty of Education at Benson Idahosa University.

She has ministered internationally in Belfast, Ireland; Benin City, Nigeria; Stockholm, Sweden; London, England; Accra, Ghana; Juarez, Mexico; Port-au-Prince, Haiti; Leeds, England, and Meru, Kenya as well as across the United States.

Her first Vocal Recording was produced in London, England.

Gail is invited to speak at School Graduations, Singles Ministries, Missions and Women's Conferences as well as Leadership Conferences.

She currently resides in Tulsa, Oklahoma, and may be reached by e-mail at tgtali@aol.com or Facebook.

Scripture References for "Angels"

(All scriptures are taken from King James Version)

Genesis 19:1
And there came two angels to Sodom at even; and Lot sat in the gate of Sodom: and Lot seeing them rose up to meet them; and he bowed himself with his face toward the ground;

Genesis 19:15
And when the morning arose, then the angels hastened Lot, saying, Arise, take thy wife, and thy two daughters, which are here; lest thou be consumed in the iniquity of the city.

Genesis 28:12
And he dreamed, and behold a ladder set up on the earth, and the top of it reached to heaven: and behold the angels of God ascending and descending on it.

Genesis 32:1
And Jacob went on his way, and the angels of God met him.

Job 1:6
Now there was a day when the sons of God came to present themselves before the Lord, and Satan came also among them.

Job 2:1
Again there was a day when the sons of God came to present themselves before the Lord, and Satan came also among them to present himself before the Lord.

Job 38:7
When the morning stars sang together, and all the sons of God shouted for joy?

Psalm 8:5
For thou hast made him a little lower than the angels, and hast crowned him with glory and honour.

Psalm 78:25
Man did eat angels' food: he sent them meat to the full.

Psalm 78:49
He cast upon them the fierceness of his anger, wrath, and indignation, and trouble, by sending evil angels among them.

Psalm 91:11
For he shall give his angels charge over thee, to keep thee in all thy ways.

Psalm 103:20
Bless the Lord, ye his angels, that excel in strength, that do his commandments, hearkening unto the voice of his word.

Scripture References for "Angels"

Psalm 148:2
Praise ye him, all his angels: praise ye him, all his hosts.

Matthew 4:6
And saith unto him, If thou be the Son of God, cast thyself down: for it is written, He shall give his angels charge concerning thee: and in their hands they shall bear thee up, lest at any time thou dash thy foot against a stone.

Matthew 4:11
Then the devil leaveth him, and, behold, angels came and ministered unto him.

Matthew 13:41
The Son of man shall send forth his angels, and they shall gather out of his kingdom all things that offend, and them which do iniquity;

Matthew 13:49
So shall it be at the end of the world: the angels shall come forth, and sever the wicked from among the just,

Matthew 16:27
For the Son of man shall come in the glory of his Father with his angels; and then he shall reward every man according to his works.

Matthew 18:10
Take heed that ye despise not one of these little ones;
for I say unto you, That in heaven their angels do always behold the face of my Father which is in heaven.

Matthew 22:30
For in the resurrection they neither marry,
nor are given in marriage, but are as the angels of God in heaven.

Matthew 24:31
And he shall send his angels with a great sound of a trumpet, and they shall gather together his elect from the four winds, from one end of heaven to the other.

Matthew 24:36
But of that day and hour knoweth no man, no, not the angels of heaven, but my Father only.

Matthew 25:31
When the Son of man shall come in his glory, and all the holy angels with him, then shall he sit upon the throne of his glory:

1 Corinthians 6:3
Know ye not that we shall judge angels?
how much more things that pertain to this life?

Scripture References for "Angels"

1 Corinthians 13:1
Though I speak with the tongues of men and of angels, and have not charity, I am become as sounding brass, or a tinkling cymbal.

Hebrews 1:6
And again, when he bringeth in the firstbegotten into the world, he saith, And let all the angels of God worship him.

Hebrews 1:7
And of the angels he saith, Who maketh his angels spirits, and his ministers a flame of fire.

Hebrews 2:7
Thou madest him a little lower than the angels; thou crownedst him with glory and honour, and didst set him over the works of thy hands:

Hebrews 12:22
But ye are come unto mount Sion, and unto the city of the living God, the heavenly Jerusalem, and to an innumerable company of angels,

Hebrews 13:2
Be not forgetful to entertain strangers: for thereby some have entertained angels unawares.

2 Peter 2:4
For if God spared not the angels that sinned, but cast them down to hell, and delivered them into chains of darkness, to be reserved unto judgment;

2 Peter 2:11
Whereas angels, which are greater in power and might, bring not railing accusation against them before the Lord.

Jude 1:6
And the angels which kept not their first estate, but left their own habitation, he hath reserved in everlasting chains under darkness unto the judgment of the great day.

Revelation 1:20
The mystery of the seven stars which thou sawest in my right hand, and the seven golden candlesticks. The seven stars are the angels of the seven churches: and the seven candlesticks which thou sawest are the seven churches.

Revelation 3:5
He that overcometh, the same shall be clothed in white raiment; and I will not blot out his name out of the book of life, but I will confess his name before my Father, and before his angels.

Scripture References for "Angels"

Revelation 7:1
*And after these things I saw four angels standing on the four corners of the earth, holding the four winds of the earth, that the wind should not blow on the earth,
nor on the sea, nor on any tree.*

Revelation 7:2
And I saw another angel ascending from the east, having the seal of the living God: and he cried with a loud voice to the four angels, to whom it was given to hurt the earth and the sea,

Revelation 7:11
And all the angels stood round about the throne, and about the elders and the four beasts, and fell before the throne on their faces, and worshipped God,

Revelation 8:2
And I saw the seven angels which stood before God; and to them were given seven trumpets.

Revelation 8:6
And the seven angels which had the seven trumpets prepared themselves to sound.

Revelation 8:13
And I beheld, and heard an angel flying through the midst of heaven, saying with a loud voice, Woe, woe, woe, to the inhabiters

of the earth by reason of the other voices of the trumpet of the three angels, which are yet to sound!

Revelation 9:14
Saying to the sixth angel which had the trumpet, Loose the four angels which are bound in the great river Euphrates.

Revelation 12:7
And there was war in heaven: Michael and his angels fought against the dragon; and the dragon fought and his angels,

Revelation 12:9
And the great dragon was cast out, that old serpent, called the Devil, and Satan, which deceiveth the whole world: he was cast out into the earth, and his angels were cast out with him.

Revelation 14:10
The same shall drink of the wine of the wrath of God, which is poured out without mixture into the cup of his indignation; and he shall be tormented with fire and brimstone in the presence of the holy angels, and in the presence of the Lamb:

Revelation 15:1
And I saw another sign in heaven, great and marvellous, seven angels having the seven last plagues; for in them is filled up the wrath of God.

Scripture References for "Angels"

Revelation 15:6
And the seven angels came out of the temple, having the seven plagues, clothed in pure and white linen, and having their breasts girded with golden girdles.

Revelation 15:7
And one of the four beasts gave unto the seven angels seven golden vials full of the wrath of God, who liveth for ever and ever.

Revelation 15:8
And the temple was filled with smoke from the glory of God, and from his power; and no man was able to enter into the temple, till the seven plagues of the seven angels were fulfilled.

Revelation 16:1
And I heard a great voice out of the temple saying to the seven angels, Go your ways, and pour out the vials of the wrath of God upon the earth.

Revelation 17:1
And there came one of the seven angels which had the seven vials, and talked with me, saying unto me, Come hither; I will shew unto thee the judgment of the great whore that sitteth upon many waters:

Revelation 21:9
And there came unto me one of the seven angels which had the seven vials full of the seven last plagues, and talked with me, saying, Come hither, I will shew thee the bride, the Lamb's wife.

Revelation 21:12
And had a wall great and high, and had twelve gates, and at the gates twelve angels, and names written thereon, which are the names of the twelve tribes of the children of Israel: